JOY FOR YOUR
HEART

CHRISTIAN ART
PUBLISHERS

Contents

Your *Today.*
Your Tomorrow.

When we were little, we lived carefree lives. There was always someone there to protect us, guide us and look after us. But now we are all grown up …

Now we are the caretakers: of ourselves and often many others. Of course this freedom and independence is wonderful, but there are times when we long for someone to hold our hand, shelter us under their wings and show us the way.

This is especially so when we feel uncertain about the future and wonder what tomorrow will bring; times when we remember all our obligations and unresolved issues; when the challenges of life scare us a little …

In such times we need to become still before God's Word so that we can hear again:

GOD guards you from every evil, He guards your very life (Psalm 121:7).

We need to ask the Holy Spirit to engrave His promises on our hearts once more and make us realize that He, our great God, will never leave us.

> Psalm 121:8 promises, "The LORD keeps watch over you as you come and go, both now and forever."

God already has tomorrow in His hands.

Therefore we can, despite the insecurities in our hearts, take on a new year or new phase in our lives with confidence. God is good. And because of this we can look forward with great expectation to what He wants to give us. God lives. We can walk into the future with passion and freedom, knowing that
He will look after us.

Soul Mate

Father, it's not always fun
being an adult ...
Sometimes I secretly long for someone
to carry my load,
to take my hand and tell me,
"This is the way.
Walk in it."

Every day, please be
more than a someone to me.
Be **my soul mate,**
the person who has my back.
Open my eyes
to what life has to offer,
and hold me
ever so close.

His Dwelling Place –
Your Heart

Bewildered, lost and despondent, the disciples stared at the clouds. Moments before, their Master was still with them. Now He was gone forever. And they were left behind … or so the disciples thought when Jesus ascended to heaven. They had only to wait until Pentecost when the Holy Spirit Himself came down and made His dwelling place among them. It was then, probably for the first time, that they experienced God's omnipresence. Now they could live boldly as His followers.

Today, two thousand years later, the Holy Spirit still lives in each of Jesus' followers. And in you. God walks with you, throughout the year and into eternity.

This gives us reason to truly live with heart and *soul*.

❝ And be sure of this:
I am with you **always**,
even to the *end*
of the age. ❞

Matthew 28:20

2

Rest in Who *You Are*

We can easily convince ourselves that there are many important things on our to-do list. And then we feel so guilty for not doing them that, over time, we forget how to really enjoy life.

You are chosen. You are a unique person, made by Your Creator with great care and attention to detail. There is no one on earth quite like you. Your appearance, thoughts and behavior are uniquely you. Your talents, gifts, personality, drive, likes and dislikes are distinctly yours.

We know this, but still we try very hard to measure up to the world's ideal image. We so wish to be and look like someone else and go to great lengths to be accepted by others. There's nothing wrong with wanting to be the best you can be – healthy introspection and good habits never hurt anyone. But remember, because each person is unique, our Creator doesn't expect a "one-way-fits-all" way of living from us.

> Jesus said to her,
> "Your faith is great.
> Your request is
> granted."

Matthew 15:28

Rather, He wants to see how we develop, live and enjoy our uniqueness within certain boundaries.

It's wonderful to start a new year with positive resolutions. But follow them without comparing yourself to others, and without punishing yourself for the things you did or didn't do.

Let God show you who you are and especially who you can be through Him. This year, decide to appreciate your life as a child of God, and to become more of who you are and more like Him. {Remember, He loves you ... just the way you are!}

Blessed and Highly Favored

She was a gentile woman. But still she called out to Him. She believed that He could save her child who was possessed by demons.

Somewhere in this Canaanite woman's soul, which we read of in Matthew 15:21-28, she knew something of Jesus' mercy for all people and His limitless love. "Let a little piece of Your mercy fall upon me," she pleaded.

Then we read how Jesus admired her childlike faith, and He granted her request. God can use any person. He looks for people who acknowledge their dependence on Him, and humbly bow before Him and ask for His grace. Such people are His chosen ones. They are good enough – just the way they are.

Free

I tire myself out, Lord,

because I believe

that I must be different,

I must do more,

I must look better.

Today I realize that

this tendency to be perfect

doesn't come from You.

Please heal me of this

self-imposed "must-be" syndrome

so that I can be free

to just be my own person.

3

Journey of Love

We all want to be loved, because love has a way of covering our hearts like a blanket, and making us feel secure.

Without love, we become cold and hard, and we feel abandoned … we struggle to really live.

The fact is, God loves each one of us. In His heart is infinite and unconditional love for every person on earth.

He loves us even when we are on the path of falsehood, and feel abandoned, guilty or inferior. He loves us when we are far from Him and we wonder how He can ever love us.

He loves us when other people's words and actions remind us why we don't deserve to be loved.

He loves us when we stand vulnerable before Him and confess that we are nothing without Him, that we are in desperate need of His mercy.

To grasp God's love for us is a lifelong journey, a daily walk-with-Him road; a go-astray-and-find-the-way path; a forget-and-remember journey … It is a road where we must allow the Spirit to reveal the truth to us. This is the truth that states that –

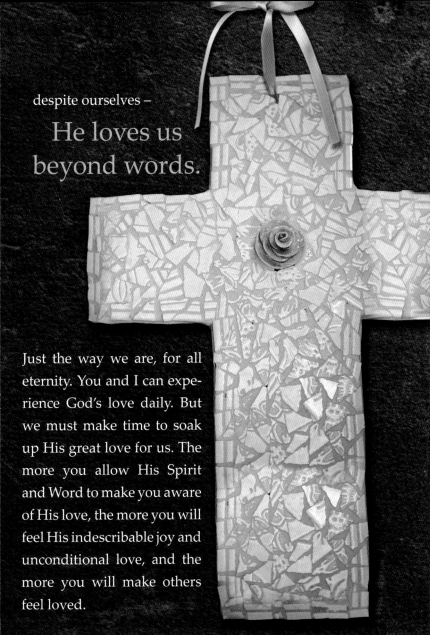

despite ourselves –

He loves us
beyond words.

Just the way we are, for all
eternity. You and I can experience God's love daily. But
we must make time to soak
up His great love for us. The
more you allow His Spirit
and Word to make you aware
of His love, the more you will
feel His indescribable joy and
unconditional love, and the
more you will make others
feel loved.

Just the Way You Are

One after the other he baptized them, committed to his task of preparing the way for the Messiah. Then one day Jesus Himself stood before John and asked to be baptized. And when the heavens opened and God declared that this was His beloved Son, John knew what a great privilege it was to be a forerunner of Love.

You are baptized in His love. Remember this every day and be a forerunner of His great love. Yes, live as His beloved child, just the way you are, forever.

> The LORD *delights in you* and will claim you as His bride. Your children will commit themselves to you, O Jerusalem, just as a young man commits himself to his bride. Then God will rejoice over you as a bridegroom rejoices over his bride.

Isaiah 62:4-5

Brimming over with Love

Heavenly Father,
it is sometimes hard to believe
that You love me just the way I am.
Thank You so much for that!

Every moment of every day
I want to live in the truth
of Your love for me, Father.
Help me to make time
to hear it, to receive it, to experience it,
and to make it my own.

Fill me with Your godly love
in such a way
that I will live it out spontaneously.
Let the truth of love
flow from me constantly,
because I received it so abundantly.

4

Be Still and Know ...

God's roadmap for our lives is
sometimes difficult to understand,
but is always trustworthy.

When you look back on your life, it will be unmistakably clear that your path did not always turn out like you planned or hoped.

There might have been times when you dreamed of something, but it turned out to be a disaster. At other times your path crisscrossed before you reached your destination. And then there might have been times when the detours of life left you hopelessly lost and you wondered if God's plan still made sense.

The truth is that God knows – regardless of our own hopes and dreams – what is best for us. Yes, He knows – despite our impatience – the right time for the right things.

God knows every little detail of your life, your expectations and your thoughts. He understands your disappointments and your questions. He has compassion with your "What now, Lord?" disbelief. But He also knows when it's time for a detour; when He needs you to change direction or wait … just for a little while.

Always be sensitive to the Father's voice in all circumstances. Be willing to trust Him and prepared to follow where He leads. He always wants what's best for you.

Today, become still before Him and listen when He says:

"Be still and know
that I am God!
I will be honored
by every nation.
I will be honored
throughout the world."
The LORD of Heaven's Armies
is here among us;
the God of Israel
is our fortress.

(Psalm 46:10-11)

There's Direction in Your Journey

The Joseph history is a typical detour story. He hoped to get special treatment as his father's blue-eyed boy, but instead was taken to Egypt as a slave. When he tried with all his might to do the right thing, he was accused of adultery and thrown in jail. There he interpreted the dreams of the cup-bearer and the baker, and hoped for two long years to be set free.

How cruel and bizarre the situation seemed … until God's perfect plan became clear. Joseph became governor and worked out a brilliant strategy that saved thousands of people from starvation (see Genesis 37-41).

God's detour stories often have surprising endings.

Just trust Him with yours.

God's GPS

Lord, sometimes
I don't understand
and I even wonder
if You still care about me;
if You still hear my heart.

Today Your Spirit
reminds me afresh
of the truth
that You are in control:
of world events
and their outcome …
and of my life.

Help me to hold
tightly on to You,
to trust You,
and to know:
You will always hold me
close to Your heart.
You will always
enfold me in
Your love.

He is our God forever
and ever,
and He will guide us
until we die.

Psalm 48:14

5

Do You know *Me?*

When the blood of the Lamb is smeared on the

frame of your heart, you can know for certain

that eternal death will pass by your door.

You will live for
all eternity with God!

The Israelites' instructions were strange: They were to smear a lamb's blood on the doorframes of their houses. Then God would pass by their homes that night when all the firstborn Egyptian sons were killed. The Israelites would be spared.

How wonderful that the Lamb's blood is also available to us. We have the choice of smearing His blood on the frames of our hearts.

If you have accepted His great love for you, and allowed His blood to free you, you can be assured that He has chosen you. Eternal death will forever pass you by. You will live with Him for all eternity!

Let us bow down every day with gratitude before our Redeemer, because He delivered us with His blood on the cross while we were still in chains. Let us then live with renewed joy, knowing that our lives are sealed by His love, *now and always.*

Thank You for Life

Redeemer of my life,
if You had not come to earth
I would have been lost forever.
If You had not died for our sins,
I would have had to pay for mine.
If You did not rise again,
death would be
horrifying for all of us.

But You came
to paint my heart with Your love
so that I could live a redeemed life.

Dear Lamb of God,
thank You for not passing me by
when you freely gave Your grace.
Today I take hold of life again
with immense gratitude.

Write Sunday on
Your Heart

Dark were the hearts of Jesus' friends that fateful Friday. To lose their Master and Friend and to see Him on the cross tore their hearts apart. Perplexed and lost, they wondered if this was the end of the salvation plan … until that Sunday morning when they heard that their Lord was not dead, but alive!

Their sorrow turned to utter joy when they realized that the end of the road was only the beginning of a new life …

God's road has no dead-end streets. When our hearts acknowledge Him, we receive new mercies, new hope and new life from Him every morning.

Do you know Him in such a way?

" The blood on your doorposts will serve as a sign, marking the houses where you are staying. When I see the blood, I will pass over you. This plague of death will not touch you when I strike the land of Egypt. "

Exodus 12:13

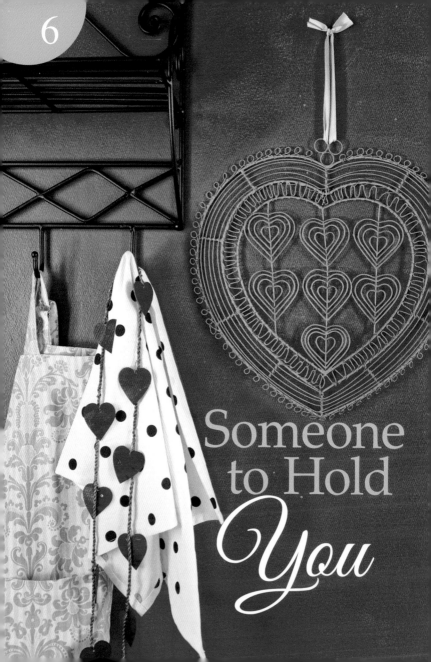

6

Someone
to Hold
You

Someone once said that a mother always has your back. When the world abandons you, and you look back, she will still be right behind you.

A mother is so different: She believes in her children no matter what … even when they disappoint her; even when they mess up and are not nearly perfect. With her you can sit barefoot at the kitchen table and talk about anything. She's like a big tree underneath which you can lie down and be shaded from the sun. And in the cold of winter, a mother is like a cozy fireplace where you can warm yourself.

Mothers teach us something about the heart of our Father: the heart where we are always welcome and where we can just *be*. God knows us, and so do mothers. They know what's brewing inside our hearts long before we say a word about it. They share our joys and sorrows, and comfort us when we search for answers. God made mothers so that we could experience His unconditional love through the heart of a mere human. He gave them to us so that we can experience a little bit of

heaven on earth.

Through a mother we can feel something of God's mercy and love in her safe arms, so that we can return "home" when we need some TLC.

Let us honor each and every mom on a regular basis – the moms who are still with us and those who are already sitting by the Father's throne, praying for us. Let us praise our Father, because through His Son we can look forward to being in a heavenly home with Him for all eternity.

Covenant Love

Thank You, dear Father

that we can see Your greatness and love

through the heart of a mother.

Thank You for giving us

earthly homes

where we can experience

a heavenly homecoming.

Thank You especially

for the privilege of being children

of Your kingdom

through our covenant with You,

for generations to come.

A Mother's Great Task

It must have been very hard for the once-childless Hannah to give her long-awaited son, Samuel, back to God. Nevertheless, she kept her promise and took him to the temple at the right time so that he could dedicate his life to God (see 1 Samuel 1:26-28).

Mothers know that God gives us children so that we can bring them up to love Him. For this reason, mothers bow before God regularly to offer their children's souls to Him. Accordingly, we who accept Him as our Savior can look forward to that glorious day when we'll all be together at the Father's throne.

The love of the LORD remains forever
with those who fear Him.

Psalm 103:17

Covenant Love

Thank You,

dear Father, that we can see Your greatness and love through the heart of a mother.

7

Thank You, Father!

A lot is expected of men with the title "Dad," because fathers must have the ability to be both strong and gentle.

The world requires many contrasting things of the modern-day man. He must have the answer for any question, but must listen to others with great patience. He must be in control in all circumstances, but must also have a softer side.

On the day that he marries, he is asked to be the cornerstone of his home, and to nurture his wife with tenderness. He must be a manly man, but must understand the soul of a woman. When his title changes to include being a dad, the list gets even longer.

He must be the great provider, but must also be able to hear the voice of his smallest child. He must balance the family's budget, yet be able to passionately play building blocks with the kids. He must be clever and wise, skilled and discreet, have good judgment and care for others.

Being a dad demands him to be man enough to handle all these things, but also humble enough to pray in full dependence: "Father, I need You in order to pass my fatherhood degree with flying colors. Help me to show my family the way to the Father's house: with my words, through my caring, but most of all through my example, Lord."

Thanks, Dad!

O Great God,

Thank You for dads!
For fathers who can be smart
and gentle at the same time.
Fathers who can stand up
for something and stick to it.
Fathers who can show the way
and lead with kindness.

Thank You, Lord, that we can
experience something of
Your Fatherhood
through ordinary, Spirit-filled dads.
And that we can sense something
of Your protective
love for us.

We honor each and every dad
who gives more than himself
for his family:
To those who share
Your greatness, goodness
and faithfulness with us.

When Mom Needs to Fill Dad's Role, Too

Sometimes the world requires a mother to also be the father. She must cook and bake, and build bridges at the same time. She must love, guide, cry and fix.

Double-role moms need more than just prayer. They need lots of God's grace, His promises and our prayers. And sometimes … they need us: our understanding, our caring and our help.

Let us honor these moms who are forced through circumstance to also fill dad's shoes and who do this with so much dedication.

> *You parents – if your children ask for a loaf of bread, do you give them a stone instead? Or if they ask for a fish, do you give them a snake? Of course not! So if you sinful people know how to give good gifts to your children, how much more will your heavenly Father give good gifts to those who ask Him.*
>
> Matthew 7:9-11

8

It is not pleasant to see all the cracks in our "clay jar" lives. Maybe we just need to learn to see the cracks in a different way …

This is Me:
A Cracked,
Earthen Vessel

Sin and our imperfections can make us feel very despondent.

This is especially so when it concerns our character traits, habits and behaviors that are so much a part of our personalities. Things like impatience, a short temper and being judgmental … they are part of our DNA, right? And we struggle to shrug them off.

The truth is that we – irrespective of our salvation in Christ – are human and live in a fallen world. In and of ourselves we can't do much about our flaws.

Only the Holy Spirit can change or transform our inner brokenness. Only He can develop and establish a new pattern and a new way of thinking, as He moves in our lives.

We must stop trying so hard to change ourselves. We'll just keep failing!

Rather, we must allow the Spirit to reprogram us. We must allow Him in unreservedly to become a part of our mindset, thoughts and habits – our pattern of life – so that He can change us from the inside out.

When we focus on Him, we will experience deliverance. Human vessels can't fix themselves. But with the Holy Spirit we can! Let us surrender all the pieces of our being to the Perfect One and experience what He wants to do in, through and for us.

Then we will become different – a brand-new kind of different!

A Mended Jar

O Spirit of God,
You know exactly
how broken I am,
how hard I try
to cover the cracks,
and how often I'm still broken.

Thank You that I don't need to stay this way
when You live in me,
because You fix more than mere cracks.
Your Spirit transforms.

Please fill every part of my being
with Your goodness, truth and love
so that I can be
what You want me to be,
so that I can be more like You.

You're Intended to Be Free!

The apostle Paul thought, lived and acted through the Spirit. And still we read how in desperation he cried out, "I don't really understand myself, for I want to do what is right, but I don't do it. Instead, I do what I hate. I want to do what is right, but I can't" (Romans 7:15, 18).

Paul confessed his human sinfulness, but he also knew what he could be through the Holy Spirit. Therefore, even in captivity, he lived as a free man.

Let's rejoice today in the victory we have through God. Let us live as newly made vessels.

Because you belong to Him, the power of the life-giving Spirit has freed you from the power of sin that leads to death.

Romans 8:2

9

Doorstep *Grace*

Every day God gives us a package filled with **blessings.**

We must just learn to
see it and enjoy it!

Children don't always realize what their parents do for them behind the scenes. Sometimes only when we are ourselves parents do we realize what Mom and Dad sacrificed for us.

Our Father blesses us with armfuls of good things. We just don't always see them, or we take them for granted.

However, when we focus our eyes, ears and hearts on seeing the gifts from His hand, the whole world suddenly looks different.

It is then that we experience extraordinary things in the ordinary. In simple things we experience joy, and in everything that happens in and around us we see God's

hand of grace.

*T*t is then that we appreciate the gleaming rays of a new dawn; we treasure the people in our lives and in everything we see little blessings. After all, everything forms part of God's bigger picture of life … eternal life.

Joy does not depend on material things. Rather, it is to be aware of *God's goodness* in any and every situation.

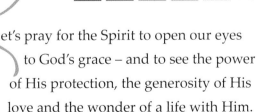

*L*et's pray for the Spirit to open our eyes to God's grace – and to see the power of His protection, the generosity of His love and the wonder of a life with Him.

Your Beloved Child

Lord, I realize
how fortunate I am.
I often don't even realize
how much I really receive from Your hand.

I thank You, Father,

for the goodness that I do see,
but especially for the things
I accept as a matter of course
and that sometimes pass me by.

Help me throughout the day

to open my eyes
to the bountiful grace and blessings that You leave
on the doorstep of my heart.

Enjoy His Blessings!

For the people who met Jesus, His life was a blessing to them. Even after His death and resurrection He still blessed them: He sheltered Mary with the gentleness of His peace, He shared His godly wisdom with the Emmaus travelers and helped His disciples to catch a record number of fish.

Today God blesses us by living in our hearts … by being a part of our daily lives. We can enjoy His presence by sharing with Him the ordinary things that happen in our lives.

May He make us sensitive to **His miracles** that so often pass us by.

LORD, You alone are my inheritance, my cup of blessing. You guard all that is mine. The land You have given me is a pleasant land.
Psalm 16:5-6

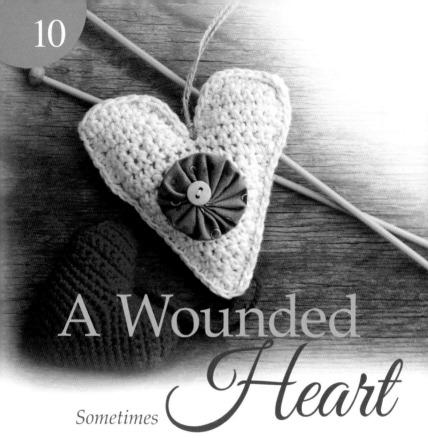

10

A Wounded *Heart*

Sometimes the poisonous arrows of people's words and actions strike our hearts deeply and painfully. And then we need to decide:

flee, fight or *forgive*.

We have all felt the sharp pain of other people's malice. Like David writes about his attackers in Psalm 64:3:

"They sharpen their tongues like swords and aim their bitter words like arrows."

When others' hurtful words and actions strike our inner being, our natural instinct is to either run away as far as possible or passionately fight back. Forgiveness is not necessarily part of our natural reaction.

The truth is that the fugitive sometimes gets lost and must return some or other time to handle the situation, while the fighter often does a lot of damage.

But those who manage to forgive … they become free! They become truly free because they remove the poisonous arrows from their hearts and allow God's Spirit of love to heal the wounds.

They become free because they leave those people in the hands of the omniscient God – knowing that God understands their motives. He loves us and wants only what's best for us.

Remember today that those who manage to let go and forgive receive so much more. They discover the wonder of peace – the kind of peace that truly brings rest to the soul … and in time helps us to love again.

The Healing Heart

Spirit of God,
You know exactly how often
we break each other's hearts,
and how hurtful this can be.
You also know how hard it is
to **forgive** like You do.

Help me, Lord,
to live as a free person,
living a life of victory
because **Your Spirit**
gives me the strength
to forgive,
to let go
and to love again.

Help me to truly be free, Lord.

You Can, Because Jesus Can!

It was a few minutes before the guards arrested Him; a few hours before Jesus would be unfairly sentenced and crucified by humankind. And still forgiveness, even under these circumstances, came naturally.

When the high priests' slaves came to capture Jesus and Peter cut off the ear of Malchus, Jesus immediately healed it.

When the world tears down, Jesus chooses to build up. When people break things to pieces, He mends. When we are lost, He saves!

How great is our forgiving God! He forgives and frees us – even when we think it's impossible.

God has spoken plainly, and I have heard it many times: Power, O God, belongs to You; unfailing love, O Lord, is yours. Surely You repay all people according to what they have done. Psalm 62:11-12

11

Your Grace Journey

Faith is not a final destination. It is a journey of grace, day by day.

The day we decide to follow our Savior, we embark on an unknown but exciting journey of faith. It is a road on which we'll enjoy soul-enriching highs and fulfilling times of peace.

Along the way we'll meet wonderful fellow pilgrims, take pleasure in God's Word, appreciate His truths and be inspired to follow the Father's will.

But the truth is that we undertake this journey of faith as fallible human beings on a path that meanders through a broken world.

For that reason, there will be times on every pilgrimage where you'll feel lost and far from God. On some days temptations will trip us up, and the demands of life will prevent us from having quiet time with God. There will be days when faith's uphill battle will just be too steep for us, and the dark depths of our emotions will leave us unsteady.

The wonderful thing is that our Father knows and understands our battle of faith, and still His unending love endures. He takes the repentant person into His arms; He equips the struggling mountaineer with His power; He searches for lost travelers, gives hope to those who are despondent and carries the heartsore believer close to His heart.

You don't need to feel dejected about *your journey* of faith, because faith is not the final destination; it is a journey that starts afresh each morning.

The Grace Traveler

Lord, I really don't feel
strong in my faith every day.
Time and time again I wonder
if I'm still on the right way.

Thank You for reassuring me today
that You'll always remain faithful …
even when I can't see the way,
and especially when I don't feel
Your presence.

Thank You that I know that
the final destination of my faith
is not today but eternity.

The Hand that Holds You …

Do you sometimes look at other believers and wonder how on earth they manage to have so much hope, belief and humility?

How about taking some time to think for a while about the men of faith in the Bible and remember how Abraham also doubted, how deceitful Jacob was, how David was tripped up by sin and how impetuous Peter denied his Master in His hour of need.

Each of God's children undertakes a unique faith journey of glory and failure, trust and doubt, and joy and sorrow. In the midst of it all, our Father remains ever faithful.

That is, after all, what faith is all about –

His grace is enough for you.

> *Not that I have already attained, or am already perfect; but I press on, that I may lay hold of that for which Christ Jesus has also laid hold of me.* Philippians 3:12

12

The Broken-Hearted Soul

A heartache needs more than special care. It needs the loving presence and compassion of our great Healer.

If we have a headache, we take medication; when we fall and our knees are scuffed, we use a Band-Aid; and when something serious is wrong, we go to the hospital.

But when our hearts are breaking, we often don't know where to turn. At times the aching is just too great for medication and bandages.

At such times it's not your best friend, the most experienced counselor, or the greatest cardiologist that can heal your pain. They can listen, comfort, give advice, and put balm on the wounds, but none of those things can make the pain disappear.

When your heart is bleeding like this, there's only one place to get relief: at the feet of the Father. This is the place where you pour out your life before Him, drink in His Word and listen quietly. You'll experience how His peace wraps around your heart like soft mist … how the pain flows out, and how His anointing sews the pieces back together one by one … and slowly but surely your heart heals.

The deeper the wound, the more time you need at the Father's feet. The bigger the hurt and the more intense the loneliness of your heartache, the richer and wider are His mercy and love.

May you always remember where to turn in your heartache. And may you find in the unity with Him how your heart heals over time – and you are able to live

whole-heartedly once again.

The Healer of My Heart

Sometimes, Lord, my heart
is broken in pieces.
In such times I just want to
cover myself in a cocoon
so that no one can
disturb me.

Thank You for knowing the
words of my heart
that I can't manage to say,
and for seeing the pain that I can't bear to watch.
Thank You for carrying me
with Your soft hand of love
until my heart is ready
to face the world again.

Thank You for being, first and foremost,
a Father to the broken-hearted …
and also to me.

Live! Because He Lives!

Can you imagine how shattered Mary was when she saw her Son's broken body on the cross? How powerless, downcast and dejected she must have felt.

And can you imagine how overjoyed she must have been when she received the news on Sunday that her Son had risen from the dead and was alive? She *knew* then: God is closer than ever on the dark Fridays of our lives. He knows how to carry us to Sunday, to the hope of a new day.

You are my lamp, O Lord;
the Lord shall enlighten my darkness.

2 Samuel 22:29

13

Jesus Prays for You!

Jesus, the Child in the manger
of old, prays for you … right now.
And tomorrow. And for always.

Jesus is born and grows into a toddler, a teenager, an adolescent. And then a man with a great calling. He experienced the loving nurturing of His mother, but also the rejection of His own people. Precious fellowship was part of His journey, but also betrayal and persecution.

Joy and peace, but also disappointment, sadness and concern were all part of the tapestry of His being.

This Jesus died, rose again and ascended to heaven where He prays for us – the people of His kingdom – daily. While we are busy with our normal day-to-day tasks, He continuously prays for us: For me. For you. For all His children. And for His church.

Because He loves you so intimately, He is with you while you're just enjoying life: while you're going about your daily errands or when you celebrate. But He's also with you in the doctor's office, in the conference room at work, and by the open grave.

He's with you when your patience runs out, when you feel depressed, scared, worried or when your heart is broken and you question the meaning of life …

Then He prays for you with the intensity of Someone who understands, because He was there once. He lived life, and came to know the world and people.

How wonderful it is that the Son of God constantly expresses our thoughts to the Father. He lifts our dreams up to Him and lovingly lays our souls before the throne of God.

My Soul Mate

Thank You, dear Lord,
for understanding my heart,
sharing my life
and for loving me so much
that You pray for me
unceasingly.

Please also pray for me
when my heart rejoices,
when I sometimes forget You
or when I don't have the words to pray.

Please grant us a new way
of hoping
in the knowledge
that You will also pray for us
tomorrow while You pave
the way there.

Our Prayer Companion

Jesus' life on earth was almost over, but He still had one important task to finish: to pray for His friends, loved ones, the church and every believer.

We read how He laid our souls before the Father with great love and pleaded for our sakes: "I pray for them. All Mine are Yours, and Yours Mine, and I am glorified in them" (John 17:9-10).

How wonderful that the Child became flesh in order to intercede for us with the Father. Now we can live as children of God without fear!

> *Who then will condemn us? No one – for Christ Jesus died for us and was raised to life for us, and He is sitting in the place of honor at God's right hand, pleading for us.*
>
> Romans 8:34

14

Live a Little

When we make time to let life flow through our souls, we experience the world very differently. And we actually live more fully.

In the fact-paced world in which we live, we can so easily let the simple joys of life pass us by. And then we miss the beauty of the things that really make us alive, like seeing the leaves of a flower and realizing that being soft and fragile is wonderful. Experiencing the majestic mountains can speak to your heart and remind you of the One who made every mountain peak. Observing a small insect makes us realize once again that we're all – however small – part of a bigger picture.

We are busy the whole year. Therefore, it's important to have some quiet time during the holidays and at Christmastime. See it as a gift from the Father's hand: a restful time to catch your breath and appreciate the simple pleasures of life again. Make time for your soul, for quiet time, for talking with your Father … for listening.

Feel the wind through your hair, drink in your surroundings and treasure the warmth of the sun on your

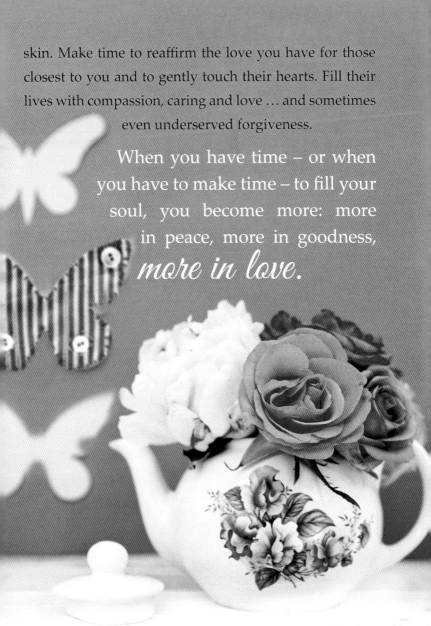

skin. Make time to reaffirm the love you have for those closest to you and to gently touch their hearts. Fill their lives with compassion, caring and love … and sometimes even underserved forgiveness.

When you have time – or when you have to make time – to fill your soul, you become more: more in peace, more in goodness, *more in love.*

Fully Human

Lord, I realize today
that I can choose
to either live a dull life
or to enjoy life to the full.

Create in me a heart that rests in You
so that I can see Your omnipotence,
experience Your goodness,
and embrace Your mercy.

Let Your love shine on me,
and Your peace dwell in me
and shine through me.

Thanks to the Light …

Her body was tired and sore, and the hay underneath her was prickly and uncomfortable. But Mary didn't complain, because in her soul burned a fire of love, through which she saw life in a different light.

She remembered how great was the God who chose her to bring His Son into the world. She remembered that this Son was to be the Savior of the world – and hers. Amidst the little that she had she experienced a piece of heaven on earth.

May the Light also illuminate your heart so that you can see the world in a new light. Enjoy every facet of it … and really *live*.

Come, see the glorious works of the Lord …
"Be still, and know that I am God!".

Psalm 46:8, 10

15

It Hurts, Lord!

Every heart has a fragile part, a part that got hurt along the way …

Do you know the wounds of your heart? Or over the years have you learned to ignore them and just live with them?

Deep hurts often happen when we are young, blindly trusting the world and people. In youth and innocence, the people we trust often do serious damage.

Some people have their hearts broken in their teenage years when they experience unkindness from their contemporaries. Other people experience the intense hurt of being rejected, or loving someone who tramples on their hearts, or later in life, losing a loved one.

Maybe you are intensely aware of the cause of your heartache, but it can also be true that a person doesn't know where the hurt and loneliness comes from.

The truth is: God knows.

He knows precisely what caused your heartache and why. And He is there to mend each broken heart and heal every wound.

He's waiting for you to open up your heart to Him so that He can show you the pain, help you deal with it and lead you to the path of complete healing.

Bring your heart unashamedly to the Father so that He can help you move past the hurt. You will find that in His healing lies deliverance, where you will discover deep

joy and
peace.

A Healed Person

Father,

I live mostly with a

fake smile.

Sometimes I just want to shout out,

"It hurts, Lord! It hurts!"

Thank You that You came

to heal broken people like me.

Today I give You permission

to touch my life with Your healing hand,

to heal the hurt,

and to fix the broken parts

that are beyond repair.

Work in me, Lord,

but please be gentle.

The Doctor of the Heart

Jesus can heal each one of us because He Himself was hurt in so many ways. He had to endure His own people's rejection and how the "clever" scribes dismissed His truths as nonsense.

Jesus longs to take care of our hearts, to heal our hurt with His gentleness and to save our brokenness through His blood. We just need enough courage to bring our hurt to Him.

His disciples deserted Him and left Him in the lurch, and He experienced the brutality of the world that nailed Him to a cross.

You have made the earth tremble; You have broken it; heal its breaches, for it is shaking. Psalm 60:2

16
Work through *Me*, Lord

God asks big things from insignificant people, because He knows we can do and be so much more.

"God will never be able to use me," you say. You're just an ordinary person who battles to always find the right words, and who's not exactly famous for your bravery.

If you think this way, you're wrong! God especially uses people who are aware of their own human frailty, weaknesses and shortcomings – in particular because when His power works through them, His omnipotence in them is unmistakable.

Yes, God gladly uses those who are big enough to set aside their own interests so that He can shape their thoughts, words and deeds, enabling them to see the true heart of the Father.

When the apostle Paul talked about himself, he didn't beat about the bush. He confessed his weaknesses, his human flaws and the things that he struggled with. Yet

it is also evident that he could look past those things because he had a vision of what Christ could do through him. Because of this, he was able to achieve so much!

If you feel small and weak, but are willing to be used by God, know this: you're excellent material for Him to work with!

If you're aware of the cracks in your armor, be glad, because then God's grace can shine through. And if you're unsure of your capabilities, remember: Your Creator rejoices over you, because He knows exactly what you can do when His greatness, goodness and wisdom work through you.

You don't have to overflow with confidence to serve Him. All that you need is an abundance of faith in God. Then small becomes … BIG. Then the voiceless receive heavenly words, and a scared heart receives courage that says, "I can, because my God can!"

Live through Me

Creator God,

thank You for who I am.

And thank You

that I'm not famous,

qualified or important.

Because now, Lord,

Your holiness can flow through me,

Your goodness can shine in me,

and You can become visible in my life.

Keep me humble enough

for Your grace, wisdom and love

to work unhindered through me.

God Has Big Dreams for You!

David was an ordinary teenager who looked after His father's sheep. And yet God chose him to be an exceptional king.

Moses wasn't a good speaker, yet this stutterer was chosen to lead the people to the Promised Land. Nehemiah rebuilt the walls of Jerusalem to honor God. All he had was a dream in his heart and total dependence on God.

Have you thought about what God could do through you if you were to come to Him in complete dependence and say, "Yes, Lord, realize Your dream through me"?

The God-of-heaven will help us succeed.
We, His servants, will start rebuilding.

Nehemiah 2:20

Doubting *Your* Faith

17

Faith is to trust even if you don't understand. And to allow God to hold you close, even though you don't see Him.

There are times when we are completely faith-orientated and are 100% convinced about what we *believe,* ecstatically happy to have God in our lives.

Then there are times when we battle to understand everything. We call out to God, but it feels like He's not listening. We get mad at Him, even asking, "Where is God when I really need Him?" To believe in God doesn't mean that you'll understand everything, receive all the answers to your questions and always feel strong in your faith. No, to really believe means that sometimes you won't understand. You won't always find answers to your questions and be at peace all the time. You'll still call out, "Father, I *know* You are with me. I accept You as my Redeemer. And I will keep searching and listening for Your voice deep inside my heart."

Faith is not about absolute answers, solutions and a life without doubt. It's also not a guarantee of a carefree, effortless existence. Faith is about putting our hope in things we cannot see, because we know that through His Spirit there is a God. This we believe even though we cannot see Him.

Faith is to hold on to the promises in God's Word, the soft voice of His Spirit and the assurance that He is with us. It is to know, even without answers, that He chose *me*.

I Know "I Am"

Sometimes, Lord, I just don't get it.

Other times I feel far away from You,

and I doubt so many things.

Then, Spirit of God, I can only ask: Pray for me

even when I don't ask You to.

Hold me close, even when I lose my grip.

Help me to believe,

because in my own strength, it's not possible.

To Believe without Seeing

The disciples were still mourning their Master's crucifixion when He suddenly stood among them and said, "Peace be with you." Thomas was not there at the time, so we can understand when he said, "No, I don't believe it." When Jesus then appeared to him and told him to touch His wounds, Thomas cried out, overwhelmed, "My Lord and my God!"

Today, two thousand years later, God is even closer to us. He lives in us and His Spirit helps us, despite our human doubt, to proclaim with conviction, "Yes, Lord, You are also my Lord and my God!"

You believe because you have seen Me. Blessed are those who believe without seeing Me. John 20:29

18

You *Are* Good Enough!

Do you appreciate being you? Or do you often wish you were someone else?

You know that you're unique. Despite having heard and read it many times, as a little child you realized that you're not like your friends. As the years went by you learned to live, work and act in a certain way.

You know that with your specific personality, talents and life experience you can do certain things well and others not so well. And that's exactly where the problem lies.

Time and time again you catch yourself wishing that you were different. Then others would admire, respect and appreciate you more, you tell yourself.

The question is not how you can be different, but how you can become more: how you, precisely as you are, can become the person God intends you to be.

Maybe it's time for you to appreciate your individuality afresh, because inside of you lies endless potential.

And the more you recognize your exceptional uniqueness and live it out through God, the more fulfilled you'll be and the more others will see the Potter's work in you.

Take a few minutes today and become quiet before your Creator. Thank Him for the person you are. Surrender your life to Him anew, so that He can use you, where you are and as you are. Then you'll blossom where you've been planted!

Thank You for Me

Creator God, forgive me for often
wanting to be someone else,
while there are so
many special talents
hidden inside of me.

Today I want to thank You
for my unique personality, talents, gifts,
background and experience.

Thank You that I'm not somebody else,
thank You that I'm *me*.
Thank You that by being who I am
others can see who You are.

You're More than Enough!

God's people were given the task of building the tabernacle. We read in Exodus 35-36 how each one stepped forward with his or her unique and special skills and offered to help with the work. And that was enough!

Because when each one gave what they had to give, there was more than enough. And God's kingdom could prosper.

God equips us with His Spirit so that we can live and prosper in our ordinary, day-to-day lives. What a privilege that we – you and I – are so unique.

Decide today to be who you are, to give what you can and to do what you can. That's all God asks of you.

And that's more than enough!

> God's filled him with the Spirit of God, in wisdom and understanding, in knowledge and all manner of workmanship. Exodus 35:31

19

Heaven
on Earth

Can one really experience heaven on earth? Or is heaven that mysterious place that we all long for, where we believe we'll end up one day?

The Word teaches us that heaven is the place where God is. It means that, when the Spirit came into our hearts, heaven was also established in us.

God is therefore not somewhere far away; He is with us where we are, every day. We smell Him in the sweet fragrance of a rose, and in the morning dew drops we see that create new life. From the cooing of a dove we know that He is close. We sense His presence in moments of silence …

Heaven is one day.

But heaven is also today. As we go about our daily grind, we know that He guides us. When we experience joy we realize that it's the heavenly rain of grace, and when we experience gentle peace in times of sorrow, we know for certain: He is still in control.

The closer we live to the Father, the more we see in our earthly journey how abundantly He blesses us with heaven – His presence. The God who lives in you also wants to show you a piece of heaven today. Is your heart ready to receive it?

A Piece of Heaven

Father God,

thank You for heaven and that I can

look forward to being together

with You forever.

Thank You also for being with me right now.

Thank You for living in me

here and now.

Please open my eyes, ears and heart

to the little pieces of heaven on earth

that You give me every day.

Help me to feel

Your presence, and to know:

This is heaven.

Someday.

But also today!

Always by My Side

Stephen was filled with the Holy Spirit. Powerfully and fearlessly he witnessed before the judgmental Jewish council. When they furiously attacked him and stoned him to death, he didn't waver, but continued to focus on God.

He wasn't afraid. He felt at peace because he didn't see the broken world, but rather God's heaven. And he knew: The Father and Son in heaven were also with him now, in his final hour.

May you see God's omnipotence in everyday things and know for certain that He loves you with an enduring love. Therefore He will never forsake you; not now, not ever.

"Heaven is my throne and earth is My footstool." Acts 7:49

20

God with *You*

It's great to know that God
wants to help us to pray. He knows
exactly what to say –
and specifically how to answer.

Sometimes we really don't have the words to say, because we're unsure of what we want to ask of God. At other times we just can't pray. It's like our thoughts are cluttered and we can't focus on the Spirit.

Then there are times when we don't want to pray because we feel guilty for not following God's will. And sometimes we are just so busy that we forget to pray!

Fortunately, our Father knows us. He knows that it doesn't always come naturally for us to talk to Him. Therefore His Spirit intercedes for us when our prayer lives aren't flourishing; when we're confused and our words get stuck in our throats. At such times He speaks on our behalf. He formulates the longings of our hearts, our cluttered thoughts and our silence and lays them gently before the Father's throne.

Our God is faithful and He gives us more than we deserve: He gives us His Word to pray from. No human language is as deep and rich as the Scriptures. When you struggle to talk to God, the Spirit and the Bible are available to help you. Let the omnipotent Holy One speak on your behalf, and let the Scriptures' perfect wisdom, supplications, praise and gratitude shape your words.

You don't always have to know what and how to pray; the Spirit and the Bible know!

Please Pray for Me

Precious Father, I love You very much,
even though it is sometimes difficult to talk to You.

Thank You for Your Spirit
who understands my heart,
sees my soul, and shapes my words in such times.

Thank You also for Your Word
from which I can pray and say,
"The Lord is with me. He helps me."

From Talking to Listening

Job served the Lord, yet God allowed him to lose everything. And of course he wrestled with His Father … questioning His actions and wanting answers. Finally, he just surrendered into the arms of his mighty God. At that moment Job confessed that he had heard about God, but had now seen Him with his own eyes.

Sometimes the most beautiful prayer is not words, but silence, at the point where we say, "Speak, Lord, Your servant is listening."

> *The moment we get tired in the waiting, God's Spirit is right alongside helping us along. If we don't know how or what to pray, it doesn't matter. He does our praying in and for us.*
>
> Romans 8:26-27